Divination with a Human Heart Attached

Poems by

Emily Stoddard

Divination with a Human Heart Attached

Cover design and layout by Alban Fischer.

Edited by Jill Boger and Josh Savory.

Formatted by Josh Savory.

www.gameoverbooks.com

I

II

III

I

They say the magpie refused shelter
in the ark, chose to stay outside
and watch
the waters rise.

More & More

The trouble is
everything calls to me.

The peacock with the red eye
glares her knowing. The red fletch
of the sandhill crane rises
like a flag in an unknown field.
The hummingbird grows large,
dances emerald infinity.

The wolf pursues the bear,
splits the shadow of pine and flashes
yellow teeth—and I do not turn away,
pursued by my own violent
reverence.

I dream of oceans and sink
to their center, into perfect squares
of coral reef. I become an oyster at work
on a precious secret. When I surface,
I gleam.

I could make the horizon pulse
with just the turn of my head.

I wake up with other languages
in my mouth: *acer negundo,*
acer negundo.

With urgent collaborations
in my throat: *magpied fields,*
magpied fields.

And I swallow every one.

Do not wake up next to me,
whispering: *Too much,*
too much.

Never say it is too much.

Tell me it is only human—
to wish for someone to believe
in the myth of you.

The Daughter Infinity

In the beginning, the sea.
In the end, the sea.

The only story, told in many ways.
The only story, tipped back and forth, old and oracle.

The generations ask for equilibrium, safe harbor.
None are ready to leave behind what's in their hands.

That's what I see.
The drowning world, full hands.

I do not have wings enough to save anyone.
I am mostly syrinx and seeing. I am the shortest path.

It has taken many floods to learn this, many more to be comfortable with it.
The daughter knew before I did. Her shadow, the longest.

Her father could not speak to her, knowing only the language of before and after.
She whispered to me about always, and again.

There are things coming that are the same thing, she said.
And she took a feather from each of my wings and dropped them into the dark.

Petronilla tries to imagine her father's prayer (I)

Peter, the leader, thus fled from every place where there was a woman. Moreover he was scandalized due to his daughter, who was very beautiful. Therefore he prayed to the Lord and she became paralyzed on one side, so that she might not be beguiled.

Acts of Philip

Which part of my body most worried him, was it the eyes

My shoulders

The cap of my elbow

What is it like, to see my body

as he once saw it

beautiful and charged

able to swing the gaze of a man and make him forget the sea

make him forget his fishing nets

make him leave everything and follow

has there ever been a body

like that

that hasn't been dangerous

I was running to him

in those days, god
spoke plain

spoke in fish and flower
ran to us with heavy baskets

so we could not miss him
so we would not confuse him
with lesser forms

of love

at the moment my spine
went cold
I was running to my father

the last thing I felt
was my long hair, the braid
that had come undone

what did he hear
when I collapsed at his feet

heavy body
broken lion
answered prayer

his eyes did not say

they avoided me after that
as though he heard nothing at all

Revisionist History

Loppers,
for when the
branch extends
too far

Injection,
to inoculate
the version
you want me
to believe

Tags,
to inventory species
to your liking

Disregard those
with an overstory
that looms—

  Sequoia sempervirens
  Juglans nigra
  Salix babylonica

Match,
to burn it all
before the forest
thickens with
truth

Truth,
a potent
pest

&

I am
emerald
ash borer.
Penetrating 100 years
in a single summer

I am
redwood.
Lightning strikes,
I burn

from the inside

I am
black walnut.
Cut my leaves,
I grow
a new face

You forget

History is water,
easily rerouted

Memory is a willow,
slice it clean
and still
the roots
regenerate

Petronilla tries to imagine her father's prayer (II)

He could have asked for the men's tongues to fallburn off. He could have asked for the men's eyes to burn out.the eyes of the men who looked at me. Even Salome had the imagination to ask for John's head on a platter. The prayer he chose for me was not cruel—it was just the most he could imagine. When they told me how he denied, I was not surprised. When they told me, I crowed and crowed and crowed.

Inheritance Rosarium

As a girl, my mother overheard her grandmother praying
to die.

> Every night after, the little girl composed
> counterweight prayers of *live, live, live.*

Twenty years later, I was born
and they still walked this tightrope together:,

> my great-grandmother having no idea
> god preferred the sound of my mother's voice.

I was one of my mother's living novenas, not baptized
in the church but in the chapel of the nursing home

> where my great-grandmother waited.

*

As a girl, my grandmother told me when a loved one neared death
she saw black crosses and waited for the phone to ring.

> Death was always near us and crossing itself.
> Even as I write this, a vulture

circles the sky to the east. I had called my grandmother
on the day she died, but I saw no crosses.

> On the night of her birthday, she slipped away
> in her sleep without warning, a perfect circle.

When I doubt the possibility of mercy, I think of her death.
The gone-to-sleep death, given to those who fear it most.

My death won't be like that.

*

I was baptized under death's wing, as a girl
born on a Friday, the day of sorrowful mysteries.

      I was a Lent-hearted girl: prone to biting my lip too hard
      just to taste the salt, loved most the day the saints

had gone to gallows. Lent was a gallery of unknowns.
St. Isidore's shovel went missing under purple folds.

      The downturn of Jesus' face became a blunt clue,
      but I always knew where St. Thérèse stood, knew

the shape of her small skull. The edges of her roses softened further
under their purple veil, as though she had chosen the dark inside

      of the darkest one and buried herself in it.

*

As a girl, I did not yet know my mother's prayers, did not know
she was born on the day of glorious mysteries, that every night

      she wove a net of *live* under a woman who asked to be buried.
      I watched my great-grandmother for her rosaries,

for the ropes of vein in her hands, for how she spoke in her old age.
Her mouth sucked and the tongue pattered,

and because she seemed the most holy person in my life,
that is how I tried to form my prayers.

A soft jaw and a knuckled rosary, a rose
wrapped around a demand:

show me, show me, show me

*

It's said a girl is carried inside the egg inside her not-yet-mother,
carried inside her future grandmother. My mother must have known.

As a girl, she took my hand, pressed it to her side,
and said: *Feel this.*

A single rib jutted away from the cage, a rupture
created by my heel, evidence of life.

If it's true, I waited on the tightrope of *live, live, live,*
was carried inside the black cross,

and they were carried first by the woman
who knew how to pray for death.

If it's true, if god is there at all, she kicks us from the inside.

Swoon Hypothesis

A collection of theories that claim Jesus did not die
on the cross but went unconscious and was later revived

Isn't that just how it goes, just when it's all figured out,
we've got god squared away and the body sent on its way,
someone comes in and suggests that maybe the miracle is not
a miracle but a sleight of hand by old Joe of Arimathea, a little slip
of a drug from good Dr. Luke, and god does not leave the body
behind as planned but instead dozes with it a little longer, wakes up
in the stone tomb and recovers. Like that line
in the funeral mass: *He has fallen asleep in Christ.*
That's all it was. The body Jesus simply fell asleep in the better part
of himself, the sweet unconsciousness of holding on.
Not unlike the mother I met at the retreat on non-duality,
who told me she respects whatever spirituality her children choose, but
she just wished it didn't mean they gave up on Jesus. The human
predicament—to go in search of freedom but refuse
to let its smaller heroes die on the mountain.
No one remembers the look on Mary Magdalene's face
when Thomas stuck his fingers in another man's side,
but you know it was somewhere between the squint of *There they go again*
and the glare of *Are you really going to let this happen.*
Not that she was without troubles, of course—the unfazed ones
are always hungry daughters. It's the problem of a love that requires no proof.
They want whatever their father is having but then they want to make it
in their own image. She had practiced the walk to the tomb
for months beforehand, learned every dusty stone and little rock
along the way. Everyone else could have his the death however they needed it.
It didn't matter to her. She'd kill him again, if that's what it took,
just to swoon a little more with the god inside.
She had never expected the body to begin with.

Magpie Says

After "Satan Says" by Sharon Olds

I am locked in a little oak confessional
with two small chairs and a table carved
with the chi rho, a P with an X running
through it, not to be confused
with the R with the X running through it,
not to be confused with medicine.
I am trying to confess my way out
of the center of the black eye
where the X pins me to the P, but forgive me,
it has been so long since my last confession
and I do not know how to begin.
Magpie comes to me and says, *I'll get you out.*
Say the church is a broken body. I say
the church is a broken body and Magpie
laughs and says, *It's working.*
Say the father bears no children.
Say the brother is a wolf in the tabernacle.
The father bears no children. The brother
is a wolf in the tabernacle. Something
opens and breaks when I say that.
My knees relax under my plaid skirt, inside
the black eye of the chi rho inside
the confessional.
Say the virgin and the whore
are the same sister. Say the gold ring
on your finger is a fool,
Magpie says, flitting down my arm.
I look at the gold ring, a promise
I have given to a man I have not met
or divorced yet. *Say it*, says Magpie.
I love this gold circle,
and inside it
is where I have spoken
to god and felt the shine of being known,

but now I do not know if it lives inside
or outside the black eye.
The gold ring on my finger
is a fool. The virgin and the whore
are the same sister. *And the wolf plays*
holy on the white veil. And the church closes
tight her eyes, Magpie says. And the wolf plays
holy on the white veil. And the church closes tight
her eyes. Something opens.
Magpie says, *Don't you see a lot better?*
And I do, but Magpie is so close
to my face that I see only blue
feathers, a door of blue
like grief
where once there was the carved
table, and the gold ring
is gone
and in Magpie's mouth now.
I am here to collect the parts. Give them to me
and I'll get you out.
But I love this gold circle
like a fallen home, and I do not know
how to be an exile yet. I want to be unpinned
but all of my belongings are still
on my back. *Give them to me*
and I'll get you out, Magpie says and spits
the gold ring outside the confessional,
where it rolls away, and Magpie follows
its bright shine past the altar, past
my family's favorite pew, past
the eighth station of the cross,
where one of the women looks out
at me and cries—*What are you*
still doing here?

Gallows Humor—
or, The Trouble with Kingdoms

When he approached his disciples, gathered together and seated and offering a prayer of thanksgiving over the bread, he laughed.

The Gospel of Judas

Our messiah hung on the cross for three weeks, and when his blood emptied, they slaughtered calves to replenish the effort. Our messiah has a body we can taste, and it tastes like a stamp from a distant island. Our angels have a sun devoted to their backlighting, and our devils speak only in spiked tongues. Our virgin mother completed her own hysterectomy so that none again would possess her. We enshrined her uterus and bring it out once a year to a crowd of bewildered silence. Our pope wears one of her fallopian tubes around his little finger but only touches it when asking us to trust him. Our mass is twice as long as the church on the next block, our knees are buckled in by a muscle stronger than our tongue. We have prayed the rosary for thirty-six hours with the awe and fear of meeting God, and afterward, roses bloomed under our fingernails. Our children have been baptized twice, first for the original sin, second for protection against future guilt. Our gospel has more bread, our Friday more fish, and our Bingo has two extra free spaces. We drink blood at the altar before noon and beer at the hall after. Our Ave Maria is always dressed for the occasion, and the occasion is always grief. And our Latin—our Latin sings like a wandering lamb, and the lamb is round and parable-innocent and forever crying out: *domus, domus, domus.*

Hivemind Elegy (There are Things Coming)

They tried to warn us, told us the truthteller
would speak in apples.

aAnd now the apple trees grow alien—
fully formed, but fruitless.

When we lost the garden, we did not know
it would begin with the bees.

Migration patterns may soon
become escape routes,

and already we speak of the earth like a lover
we're leaving three sleeps too late.

Mars and moon—we are on about colonies again,
the most prophetic wing in the museum of desire.

CThe children swarm to see astronauts, drones.
A cherry-red Tesla orbits like a beacon,

because we mark our heroes by the flags they plant.
Meanwhile the apple trees unseed themselves,

in quiet, the way a lover reveals her disbelief
simply by how she clears her throat.

I might have been a botanist

if they had let me stay inside
the elementary school biology class,
if I had not been sent to the chapel

to kneel when my parents worried
I was not ready for the reproductive
habits of flora and fauna

as it is, exile did what it does:
made the forbidden more ripe
and so I became a poet instead

when I finally got to see the parts,
it was everything my parents feared—
I was seduced

More, I said
Tell me your name, I said
without the restraint of a scientist,

the garden was left to green harder
and harder—formed lush and private
in my mind, where there is never any drought

the penchant trees, their xylem and phloem:
one path to carry water, another to descend
with sugar for the root

black walnut's soapy smell
and its many-chambered pith, which is enough
to know it is not the tree of heaven

flora climbs my throat, no wonder
I wake up with new roots—*datura, acer negundo*—
in my mouth

O purple stalk, my teacher now—
yesterday you were a sign of life
but today, so I've learned, you are loosestrife

and I am ripping you out
before you choke
bee balm, ironweed, boneset

O anther
O stigma
O filament

don't be mistaken:
I was loved so carefully
so tediously

like a daughter

they only forgot to ask
what I am a daughter of

The Heart Renames Itself Beholden

Because the nightshade—*datura, jimson weed, devil's snare*—
has grown now along the edge of the uplands, I have gloved my hands
before touching, I have turned to thoughts of controlled burn

Because the past is a ceiling that my dreams grow
above my head, I have turned to pre-sleep prayer as a trick,
a conjure: *Burn this, too*—

They say anything in the dream is not the thing itself
but the shard of yourself that calls the thing home—
because of this, I know something of my first marriage

is still a buried flag, an unnamed seed that turns
tansy in me, turns nightshade—*datura, datura, datura*
hangs down from the ceiling, the devil's snare

or am I reaching up toward it, matchbox in my hand?
My second husband's face never belongs to him very long but,
slips into the face of the first, a warning

that I might never unloose that first fooling—
Because of this, I worry I am not wise enough yet
to separate my hungers from my harvests

growing now along the edge of the uplands
I glove my hands before touching
the nightshade—*datura, jimson weed, devil's snare*—

I turn to thoughts of controlled burn

Where did I leave my god

I am sure my god is here somewhere, hidden
    between department store racks, tucked between
  the gold-star clearance cardigans and last season's tank tops,
like themy brother we sometimes called Houdini.

    I sometimes wished he would not be found, wished
  he would slide away into the pleated pants, far quietermore quietly
than how he arrived. Sometimes my god disappears like that,
    and I become a woman stalking the river—

  I am no sheep. I am the wolf at the perimeter. I am the parent
setting the table for the feast. I am checking the door
    whenever the bell rings, only to be disappointed
  when it's another Amazon box arriving.

My god is a long disappearing act, a Houdini with no trap door. Please
    don't ask me to look in the church again—
  itsthe vestibules are too big, the flying buttresses hyperbolic.
You cannot hide even in plain sight there.

    I used to pray it differently, imagined dressing
  in a way that might attract my god to me.
First, the plaid skirt, the starch white of my communion dress.
Then, the nun's habit, and then, no—

  the priest's chasuble. Please don't ask me to look
in the church again. I cannot dress in plain sight there,
    and I am not brave enough
  or foolish enough

to go naked
    like Francis—otherwise I would already be
  a holy person, and at last,
my god would not matter so much to me.

Instead, I keep a running joke that my neck is so long
because it's supposed to have room for a collar.
I keep a running joke, because god knows
        a joke wants to be a naked prayer—

The last time I made this joke, the phone rang, at last.
But it was my great-great-great-grandfather, the Methodist minister,
            and he said: *If you have a collar on your neck,*
    it only makes it easier for them to put a leash on you.

How long have I been stalking the river
            with my neck lowered, looking for a god
        to attach it to? And where is that god now—
who is not like my brother, who always returned

            from the clearance racks. How brutal he could be,
        the way he once stared beyond me and screamed:
god is dead god is dead god is dead
        and I did not believe him, needed to believe

the fallen angels are so bitten by god
            they can't keep the love on the inside anymore,
        so they have to deny it, run from it, hide from it—
the way it felt when my future husband tried

            loving me after I hadn't been loved for a long time.
        How bitter I was at first, how skeptical
when he thought of me: *Can I help you set up for the party?*
        Want me to bring extra wine glasses? You get to bed, I'll clean up the kitchen.

My god is something like that: the love that puts you to bed
            when you've had a little too much, disappears
        to the kitchen where the mess waits,
hates the phrase *unsung hero* just like my husband hates it,

because he insists:

It's impossible to be unsung
and recognized at the same time.

How long have I set the table, how long
have I checked the door, how long have I
attempted singing—

Let me be quiet for once, if I can
undo the collar, if I can unpin the veil.

Let the boxes stop arriving.
Let the phone stop ringing.

Let the clearance rack unpleat itself.
Let my brother stop howling for a dead god.

The wine glasses are empty.
The kitchen is clean.

I'm so full of waiting,
I might as well be lost.

II

They say the magpie was the only bird
who chose not to sing or dress
in mourning
at the crucifixion.

One for sorrow, two for joy

there was so much grief to go around

but the men could only grieve for themselves

grief too much for their bodies

so they hung it in the trees

my father to the crabapple

Judas to the redbud

even though they had been promised

something more than their bodies

even though they were only grieving

a body

but I didn't dare speak of freedom now

swallowed the magnetic blue feathers

of the magpies in my mouth

helped my mother fix

dinner for my father, while the crabapple

blossoms fell away

from the kitchen window

Sun Square Moon: An Equation as Abecedarian

I am a midwife
and a woman who does not give birth.
I am the solace of my own birth pains...

I am the sign of the letter and the indication of division.

Thunder, Perfect Mind

Arrangement of birth-day sky that points to this:
born precocial, feathered in the nest and no
chance to begin naked on the other side of the equation,
downed and dressed, already
expected to fly, expected to sing—the girl with the long
feather in her throat

Gone is the premonition my grandmother gave my mother about me,
her habit of telling futures in the gaze of newborns—
it's only right it was forgotten, buried in the point where goosebumps
join calamus to skin, a place only I can feel and try to solve for:
killdeer song that turns my own name into a warning,
lilts the stranger in me away from the nest,
moves in widening circles in the broken wing dance, but
never on both sides at once—a variable that makes me feel safer

Open hole in the ground, you never lied to me: everything worth
protecting begins in shallow dirt and plain sight, before there is time to
question the circling hawks or predict what
route the wing will take—
somewhere my grandmother remembers the promise she heard for me,
the skin before the world asked for flight—even the stars
underpin its weight, as they calculate the
violence of hawks and take solace in the division of my
wing. My sky says I have always been more
x-chaser than mother of

yearling, but teach me how to carry that—how to go undefined by the zero that was born in the hole with me.

Descendants

restless
for the language
an ancestor spoke
into the sky
of their god

we sift remnants
of tongues,
break the
breath

we count
in generations
and this is
false math

the ladder
of my spine
is lined by shores
that were not ours
to fish

by altars
where we bowed
and altars
we burned

by prayers
kept
and
killed

&

we are not done yet
inventing names
for what will save us

even now

some speak of doves
and some speak of towers

Passion Play

In the sacristy, I consider striking distance
and the angles of whips.

How close would a Roman soldider need to be
to solicit a gash? How close to createfor a hairline of red?

Would the whip roll across the skin in one clear lick,
or would it hiccup across the folds?

Did the son of the father have folds of skin,
or was he polished tight by hard work like my father?

How different are the muscles of a carpenter
from the muscles of a forester?

I decide on wide slashes—precise but hungry,
as if the soldier had wanted to peel into the heart—

and apply the blood, a mix
of Kkaro syrup and red dye.

Like Jesus in Gethsemane, my father did not want
to be Jesus. He said he wanted to be Peter.

The parish priest knew better: my father has never
not wanted to be the hero.

So every year, he carries a cross through the church,
trailed by the screams of parishioners: *Crucify him! Crucify him!*

He wears a crown of thorns he made from a wild honey locust,
and better than ash, it leaves a bloody mark on his forehead.

We raise his body up on the cross he built himself
from a redwood tree.

My mother makes the same joke about trying
to live with him when he thinks he's God,

and we practice his lines so much they become
a new kind of family prayer.

I say: *Father, if it is your will*—
My brothers cry back: *take this cup from me!*

I say: *The reason I was born,*
the reason I came into this world—

and my brothers call:
is to testify to the truth!

My father is known for his wail:
My God! My God! Why have you forsaken me?

But I covet the lines where Jesus sounds lonely
and surprised by it:

Peter, are you asleep?
Could you not watch one hour with me?

As lonely as anyone who has ever tried to be human.

Every year, I find a little more of the broken
alien inside of him—

My kingdom is not of this world.
If it were, my subjects would be fighting

to save me from being handed over.
As it is, my kingdom is not from here.

Every year, I want more passion, less resurrection.
Every year, the slashes get wider.

Dreaming in the Dark Garden

The women come one by one.

To say I don't have much time.
To say I will have to braid my own hair.
To give me keys marked *5-3-1*.

They abandon me to churches and pine trees.

No small doors, they say.

There are two things that mean the same thing.
They insist.

When I don't understand, they begin to remove my feet.

A hawk eats the heart of a penguin.
A doe nudges my palm, her collarbone exposed.
A wolf shutters the bear in its jaw.

> Which of these mean the same thing?

A fleet of hummingbirds clouds a river.
The raven's black-void beak swallows a mouse.
In the morning, I hunt feathers between the sheets.

I shoot the doe cold, and a red secret blooms
outside her chest. Over the body I whisper:
thank you, thank you, thank you

ThisIt is the worst part: not knowing
how I learned to aim so dangerously.

I cut away from my body,
again and again—

slice myself awake to numb arms
and missing feet and still

too big to fit inside the church.

Every marriage is a series of smaller marriages

like a year is a series of days rising light
out of dark, the rooster singing the oldest promise.
On our wedding night, my husband gave me
a single rose with a card that said: *To my wife.*

I turned it over, looking for more. That turn,
the end of our first marriage. It was so small,
but he had seen it. He moved closer and said:
It's just after everything that's been said today,

I figured it was all that was left to say.
If he was right, I could not say it. I had not
given him my gift yet, a journal of love notes
written in the year before our wedding.

Maybe it was foolish—to expect to be always
in the beginning of the saying, but
isn't that what marriage is, a promise to trust
the better truth of what is yet to be said?

The church had tested our compatibility before
the wedding—their idea of negotiating
with the risk of sacrament. He scored worse
for his idealism about marriage.

They said I was the realistic one. They had no idea
how much more I needed to say, how much more
I was willing to risk. A year after the wedding,
I find the journal

under a bed of dust, unread. It is all that is left to say.
Maybe it was foolish, but isn't that what sacrament is—
a promise to risk fooling, to sing over and over
the same thing as a new thing.

Preservation Principles

I once laid out my collarbone as a tripwire,
       convinced that exposure might be a kind of compromise.

*

I ate my own voice box for fear
       that it would reveal too much—

              Mute then, but the mind of the heart still assembled
                  a violent vocabulary.

       Memory is never so easily swallowed.

*

I ate your pain like a rock unpolished—

       Cracked open my wrists so you could see I am real,
          human like you. But your hands are soft.

       They've never callused. You don't take to calluses.

              And your teeth—
              Untrained for rock.

*

Now I drag my tongue like a rotting fish through salt.

          Where were you while I was dismantling myself?

       Here is my body, open and uncured.

          You were never going to stitch me back together.

Wait for It (Three for a Girl)

The Passion according to Petronilla
After Jane Kenyon / After Terrance Hayes

My father falls asleep in the garden. This is how I learn god
has a sense of humor. My father falls asleep in the garden, and he does
remember the buttercups, but he does not

remember the arrival of soldiers or the locusts taking leave
of their chafing just before. This is how I know god is waiting for us
to hear the punch line, the dry and comfortless

laugh reserved for the man late to his own story. So
humoroused god is, he gives my father three more chances to let
the ending go otherwise. After that evening,

the dreams come—a woman carrying 153 fish, who tells me: don't
be afraid. Every morning after, I clean my father's net, let
the linen slip between my hands and spread it out to dry. In the evening,

I refasten each of the stones and test the weight of what's to come.
When my father finds me bent to the work, I want to say: don't
be afraid,

but he is not ready yet. *Those with ears, let them hear.*
My father is prone to striking off what he doesn't understand., Tthe ear
of the boy in the garden is an impulse I know well.

So I am surprised when he comes to me and says he will let
me join them on the boat. I don't know what he dreams, but that morning
on the water, I am ready for the words that come:

Friends, haven't you caught any fish? My father tries to hear
the man on the shore, but it's just as well
he doesn't catch the joke, as the slap of fish fills the ear.

We eat well that night. My mother lights every candle. We let
every spot at the table be filled with a guest. It's long after evening
when I hear the footsteps of soldiers. Now they have come

43

to collect my father. He is telling a story and goes dead silent. Tomorrow, I will clean the net again, refasten the stones. But tonight, my mother laughs. She kisses his ear. She says: don't be afraid.

Divination with a Human Heart Attached

You know the story: The son returns, and now, a feast.
The brother reanimates, whole again. The daughter resurfaces,
and with her, flowers. All retrieved from a supernatural place,
but not

for any supernatural reason. Only because someone needed them,
and grief is too much. Miracles that are more human upon inspection.
You know the story: the children are restless in the garden,
but not

for want of food or love. Only because no animal can perfectly
avoid itself. Even ants will begin to groom themselves if given a mirror.
They follow their own scent to find the way home again,
but not

like the robin this morning, colliding with the window, tempted
by a misplaced reflection. WUpon watching her collapse in the dirt,
the first instinct was a tenderness: Would she fly again?
But the answer was hungry and familiar: With these wings, what omen?

Rooster Litany

Daughters of Jerusalem, weep not over me; but weep for yourselves, and for your children... For if in the green wood they do these things, what shall be done in the dry?

Luke 23:31

What shall be done, and how long will we dress in purple

     What shall be done, and why does the priest wear green

What shall be done, and still the priest says, Take this. Eat.

This, broken on our bodies

     This, broken on our children's bodies

This, on our grandparent's bodies

        but they could not tell us

Broken body, but the basket still passes whole

     Broken body—what shall be done, now that our songs go dry

Broken body, what could "The City of God" give

our children

     who will not be lullabied back

          from the mass grave in Ireland

our children

     who will not be lullabied back

          from the attic in Vermont

our children

     who will not be lullabied back

          from the confessional in Montreal

our children

     who will not be lullabied back

          from the room in Igloolik

our children

     who will not be lullabied back

          from the rectory in Pennsylvania

     what shall be done, when we will not be lullabied—

O god, remember

your promise: to remember

every denial

made a cornerstone.

O god,

only the rooster

feels better

when he sings.

O god,

for every child:

a rooster to crow.

for every child:

a rooster to crow.

for every child:

a rooster to crow.

Four for a Boy: These Things in Her Heart

I.

Host uterus.
Someday there would be other names,
more gracious names
for it, but I'll be honest:
I was only a girl
when I heard the voice,
a girl with hardly any voice
of my own, except for the one
I lodged withat god every night.
He was the one I spoke to most freely,
having been promised to him
as a condition of my own arrival,
and so he must have been the one
who knew me best
and maybe even took pity on me
in my loneliness,
and brought me a gift.
I thought the baby was only for me
at first. How quickly he filled me,
how complete my prayers
after that.

II.

It's easier to accept an unexpected baby
after the baby is born.
Before, only the mother knows how easy
it is to love the unknown, because the unknown
kicks inside of her and wakes her up
at night and responds to her voice.
After, the baby belongs to everyone
because he wants to survive,
and so he smiles for his uncles

in a way that makes them share their food,
and he laughs in a way that makes strangers
forgive his curious arrival, and he claps
his tender, new hands together
until his grandmother picks him up.
How quickly he belonged to everyone,
how outside-myself my prayers became.

III.

My mother always teased me: *That baby takes care of you*,
which I think about the first time we lose him
and he's bothered by how worried
I am. "Why were you searching for me?" he asks,
but I hear it, inside the words: *Why do you need me so much?*
He is outgrowing me, has always been outgrowing me.
I did not know that becoming a mother
would be a series of departures, that the choice
had been made for me
as soon as a stranger's hand sliced
the tether between us.

IV.

For forty nights I dream of fire
and the single, silent bird.
No sound except the hot wind and his voice,
over and over again:
Why were you searching for me?
Why were you searching for me?
Why were you searching for me?
On the fortieth night, the bird
leads me to a nest, and it is there—
between the collection of silver pieces,
frankincense, and gold coins: the white cord,

coiled in the center of the nest like a snake.
A gift.
This is god's language. I am older now,
I recognize it.
The bird looks at me.
The fire is coming.
It is my choice.
At last, I shake my head.
The bird perches, takes the cord into his beak,
swallows it whole.

III

They say the devil left a drop of blood under
the magpie's tongue. They say the magpie has a long
memory for faces, remembers the good ones apart
from the bad, can recognize her own
in the mirror.

Five for silver, six for gold

I'm a good daughter, but I'd rather be a gilded wing.

In St. Peter's, my husband wonders: *What's up with the flaming bird?* And I do not answer, ashamed of the sudden sacrilege I feel on his behalf.

Weighted coin in my throat, that old cathedral loyalty. Tapestry and chalice. Incense and marble. Indulgences I try to be more wary of, even as I rummage their bodies for something to mark the stranger in my own.

I'm a good daughter, but I still knock on heavy doors and expect doves to answer.

I'm a good daughter, but I'd rather be a heart bursting into flames.

It embarrasses me, to see myself

in the god exhibit. How it circuses and exaggerates every color
and every color's centrifugal weight in shadows. Every rainbow
is catalogued with its preceding storm, and the omens are a series
of dead birds and fallen trees, each one tagged with a number
before it becomes kindling for the fire, which is always chewing on
the next dark possibility. Not everything is meant to be symbolic
but everything keeps trying to take the shape of a place I have loved.
There is a sugar maple being reassembled by the carpenter ants
that meant to destroy it;, the bits of bark and pith fly toward the trunk
like a firework in reverse. And as the branches return, they point to the blue
that is left behind after New Mexico clouds punch out the sky, clouds
that thin out into the San Francisco dusk that reminds me of cotton candy
being dissolved, making beautiful that feeling I could not escape,
and when I remember the feeling, its counterweight soon appears
and thickens above Lake Michigan as a blood orange curtain good-nighting
the day. The visitors *aaaahhhh* at this, and someone always chirps:
Red sky at night, sailor's delight. These syllables fill a well somewhere in the Midwest
with fireflies, which eventually causes the bur oak to flare out
and drop her acorns. The whole exhibit is one infinite Rube Goldberg machine,
and the hummingbird is the docent, of course, because nothing
is too on-the-nose or too cliché here. And it is just this lack of restraint
that embarrasses me—the overtness of the machinations, how optimistically
some people use the word *faith*. I avoid the word now, but
the joke is on me. I wake up in another hemisphere and find the magpie
singing to me on a rented porch, reminding me of the unnamed river
that prevents me from leaving the exhibit entirely. There is a single salmon
in the river that no one ever catches, and they say the final feat
is when the machine turns and runs upstream.
The final feat is always returning home.
There are saints who know the way: Francis juggling naked
in the corner of the garden, Teresa touching her heart
on the fainting couch and begging, *come closer.*
But they don't realize they are on display, and so I'm embarrassed when I gawk,
but I also don't try very hard to look away. In a small corner I try hard to forget,

there are things I've left behind: the engagement ring lost
in a Tennessee field during the music festival, the orchid abandoned
on the kitchen counter in the foggy apartment, the bluebird that was not
a fortune teller after all. Look inside this diorama and you will see my
uncreated futures
chase each other like marbles, the smallest one saying: *I love you regardless.*
It embarrasses me that I still need to look sometimes.
It embarrasses me how much I still need to hear it—that it's going to be okay.
Every other hour is darkness, but you can still hear the river.
Every other hour is darkness, but you can still hear the river.

Petronilla tries to imagine her father's prayer (III)

Because they say the third time's the charm

Because I do not know how many times you tried to form your prayer for me

Because I do not know if the prayer startled you when you first heard it

Because I want to know if you had to get comfortable with it

Because of the way my mother looks at me now

Because of the way she touches my side and asks *do you feel that*

Because of the way she says *cold*

Because she does not say barren

Because her eyes say barren

Because she speaks tenderly of Sarah, and laughter

Because the net of my body has been hung without tenderness

Because the net of my body wants to bear water

Because the net of my body dreams water

Because it was not about the body, but those dreams

Because of all the daughters the body carried inside of me

       dreaming those dreams

My father saw me once

Peter said to his daughter, "Now go back to your place, lie down,
and become an invalid again, for this is better for both of us."

The Acts of Peter

In those days, the men
spoke in miracles

Illusioned us
with talking dogs
and resurrected fish

I was a miracle once

The arm that slept elsewhere
came home to me

The dead corner of my mouth,
unstoned

But I did not rise,
did not speak

to the crowd that gathered,
knowing by then my silence

was itself a life.
My father grew angry,

seeing that his power to take
and his power to give

could not alter the daughter
inside of me

And so he undid the miracle,
which was what the crowd called it

The Worm

My father saw the once

I'm telling you: the soul doesn't recognize herself anymore.

St. Teresa of Ávila

Under the grey feet of Mount Sutro, dream
the dead grandfather, narrow tunnels, empty holes

become city-within-city, tenuous
as neighborhoods built on overturned ships

People will ask what happened out there,
meaningthey mean: *what went wrong?*

Avoid replyingthe reply: *doesn't the ocean bite at your ribs too?*
Try to unlearn the habit of startling people,

of speaking from the silk tomb
to those who depend on mirrors.

Consider: how the word tomb carries its hole in the center,
digs its own grave as it falls from the mouth.

People will caution against burning bridges,
meaningthey mean: *don't burn me.*

When the ocean incisors its way to marrow,
no earthly bridge reaches.

Only a good death reaches.
Consider: how the word *good* carries its holes in the center,

two balloons dressed for the birthday party,
where the only gift is the grandfather's return,

the walk to the empty hole, where he insists:
Here is everything you need.

Crabapple Elegy

They say you should hold
your breath when passing the cemetery,
but I do not fear the reach
of the dead.

When she died—Christmas morning,
an unforecasted veil of snow—
our chests were undone.
I learned the sounds a body makes

as it unhooks itself.
Each begins with breath.
Hers sounded like a metal cage
being stripped for parts, rib by rib.

Maybe the lungs are another Pandora's box.
When she died, all shapesforms of breath fell out.
The breath of *Silent Night*
sung over her body.

The hollow breath of those who said
it happened so fast, even though it didn't.
Only anger held itself—
until the following spring,

when the snow cleared and the earth no longer
dressed herself in black with us.
Anger waited for the first spring pruning,
for the weight of the chainsaw

in my father's hand.
Waited for the tender bark
of our favorite crabapple tree.
Waited for white flowers

and full bloom. Anger waited
for contrast. When the flowers stopped
their shaking, the proportion of grief
had finally found scale—

a bitter light in the kitchen
where branches once stretched, white shreds
of flowers across the yard, my father
slumped and heaving next to the fallen tree.

If I have to believe in anything

It's the pink of the coneflower that finally convinces me:
I have decided on ecstaticism.
I have decided on warm blood and salt,
on tightrope-treelines pressed into the sunset,
on the surprise of tears when the clouds are placed just-so,
on the soft pod of milkweed that hardens like a woman
about to give birth,
on the long neck of ironweed and its purple crown, alert,
on every single spot of the fawn as she passes, unaware.
I have decided to let it be
the dark joy—
my grandmother carried home to die in the living room,
the door swung open. She asks her children:
Did you see it—
Did you see the sunset on the highway
and how beautiful it was.

Later Marriage Poem (To sing over and over the same thing as a new thing)

In the woods this morning, there is no argument.

Last night is a tombstone,
today is a bouquet of flowers.

We walk in silence among bracken fern, between white oak.

He is wearing his plaid flannel shirt, the only one he owns,
meant for occasions like this. I am wishing I had brought my scarf.

We are on the edge of fall, when leaves decide to let go
or a cold wind decides for them.

Sometimes our silence is an old comfort,
easy and familiar as propping my feet next to the fire.

Sometimes our silence is a pulse,
a tenuous alarm that strings us together.

These times remind me that we are separate people.
Maybe that's why they happen at all—

to call me into my skin,
to mark the division in our fingers.

Sometimes I look at him and remember he has brown eyes.
How easily I forget—

the color stops mattering at a certain point.
It's the shadows that count.

The way, without effort, a pupil flares under the weight of recognition.

Seven for a Secret

What must have been left
in his stomach:
fish, his mother's bread, wild mint, almonds, water, wine

and a single olive pit

which I watched him swallow, remembering
what he had told me about how to know
when he returned

Eight for a Wish: Magpie's Intercession

What shall be done?

Stay outside, and loosen your sadness. Grief is the thing that says the world is real.
Listen: the shoreline unhitches herself as to flood. Watch: the tiny cottages tinker down.
Loosen your sadness like that, a clapboard pulled under the wave.
What shall be done? Providence is a shiny word. It is in the nest with me. It is the salt
on my wing. Stay outside, and do not be afraid. Every elegy triesis trying to tell the future.
I am the shortest path. You are the long shadow. Your memory might be the most beautiful thing about you. What you have resisted is true: the garden greens
harder in the eyes of her exiles.

Here, amen is not amen

You know this well, you who are also there

Hadewijch II

Home is wherever we hold

our breath the least

the white oak does not remember it differently

&

her memory is the only god I understand—

Here, *amen* is not *amen* but

the exhale through the center of moon

Say you know this too

&

we can be homesick together—

trade our histories like the trees do,

starting at the roots

These secret understories we keep,

        vast as oceans but bordered by skin—

    Let us defy it all

      &

    finding each other, become a revolution.

After all, the only real love

        is the kind that witnesses—

    the way a full moon shreds the forest open

          without crushing the ferns,

    a light that breathes

    &

    breathes

Sources

The research of Meghan Henning, Ph.D., provided cultural context and a historical footing for meeting Petronilla in these poems in this collection. Specifically:

"Paralysis and Sexuality in Medical Literature and 'the Acts of Peter'" (University of Dayton, Religious Studies Faculty Publications, Fall 2015)

"Chreia Elaboration and the Un-healing of Peter's Daughter: Rhetorical Analysis as a Clue to Understanding the Development of a Petrine Tradition" (Journal of Early Christian Studies, Volume 24, Number 2, Summer 2016)

"One for sorrow, two for joy, three for a girl, four for a boy..." and so on is a traditional nursery rhyme about magpies, first recorded in the 1700s by John Brand.

"Magpie Says" is based on the shape of and phrases from "Satan Says" by Sharon Olds.

The epigraph of "Petronilla tries to imagine her father's prayer (I)" comes from the Acts of Philip, as quoted in "The daughter of St. Peter" (Giovanni Maria Vian, L'Osservatore Romano, May 2014).

The epigraph of "Gallows Humor—or, The Trouble with Kingdoms" comes from "The Gospel of Judas" in The Nag Hammadi Scriptures: The International Edition, edited by Marvin Meyer.

The epigraph of "Sun Square Moon" comes from "Thunder, Perfect Mind" in The Nag Hammadi Scriptures: The International Edition, edited by Marvin Meyer.

"Wait for It (Three for a Girl)" is a modified golden shovel with lines from Jane Kenyon's "Let Evening Come." The golden shovel is a form created by Terrance Hayes in honor of Gwendolyn Brooks.

The epigraph of "The Worm" comes from The Interior Castle, as translated by Mirabai Starr.

The epigraph of "Here, amen is not amen" comes from an untitled poem by Hadewijch II, as translated by Jane Hirshfield in the anthology Women in Praise of the Sacred.

With gratitude to the editors of these publications for publishing the following poems, sometimes in earlier versions and with different titles:

America	"Passion Play"
Baltimore Review	"Inheritance Rosarium"
Cold Mountain Review	"Here, amen is not amen"
Dark Mountain	"Hivemind Elegy (There are Things Coming)"
Eco Theo Review	"I might have been a botanist"
Jarfly	"Crabapple Elegy"
Menacing Hedge	"Preservation Principles" "Revisionist History"
Radar	"I was running to him" "One for sorrow, two for joy"
Rivet	"Gallows Humor—or, the Trouble with Kingdoms"
Ruminate	"Descendants"
Rust+Moth	"Second Marriage Poem (To sing over and over the same thing as a new thing)"
Tinderbox Poetry Journal	"More & More"
Tupelo Quarterly	"Divination with a Human Heart Attached"
Voices	"If I have to believe in anything"

Gratitudes

Thank you to the ancestors who helped me listen, even when I said I didn't want to write this book. Thank you, Papa.

Thank you to Tania de Sostoa-McCue, for every 9:17 and for all these years of writing and obsessing.

Thank you to the teachers and workshop leaders who helped me find my way to this book, especially Adela Beckman, Diane Wakoski, Kelli Rusell Agodon, Susan Rich, and Marge Piercy. Special thanks to Traci Brimhall for sparking "Inheritance Rosarium" and for the gift of its title. Deep gratitude to Jenn Givhan for sharing her bright light with this book.

I'm grateful for Pat Schneider and the gifts she left us in the Amherst Writers & Artists community. Thank you to my trainers in this writing method: Maureen Buchanan Jones, Sue Reynolds, and Aaron Zimmerman—you helped me begin again at a time when I really needed it.

Thank you to the circle of writers at Voice & Vessel, for letting me be a part of your writing life and inspiring me to take creative risks in my own. Very special thanks to members of the revision circle, who responded to early drafts of some of these poems.

Thank you to friends who offered encouragement during the publishing process, especially DeDe Esque, Caitlin Townsend Lamb, and Kristin Brace. Thank you to those who held space for me in many other life-giving ways: Emily Huffman, Beth Townsend, Kate Block, Mindy Hills, Melissa Muir, and Mariaelena Welch.

Thank you to the publishing team: Game Over Books—especially Josh, MJ, and my editor, Jill—for your care with my work. Alban Fischer, for designing a cover that makes me proud to send this book out to find its people. Cassie Mannes Murray and Zoe-Aline Howard, for your wholehearted enthusiasm and support.

Thank you to my family, especially for long dinners that give way to re-enactments of the Passion Play. Thank you for driving the van in whatever direction my writing pointed next.

And to my love, Carl—sorry, I decided not to have a shit list after all. Thank you for mutual solitude and for every conversation that has involved an invisible thread, a flaming bird, or a church called St. Thomas the Dragon. I'm so glad it's you.

Biography

Emily Stoddard (she/her) is a poet and creative nonfiction writer in Michigan. Divination with a Human Heart Attached is her debut poetry collection. The book was a finalist for the Orison Poetry Prize, Wren Poetry Prize, and Barry Spacks Poetry Prize.

Emily's writing can also be found in Tupelo Quarterly, Baltimore Review, Ruminate, Radar, Tinderbox Poetry Journal, Whitefish Review, and elsewhere. In 2021, she received the Developmental Editing Fellowship in creative nonfiction from the Kenyon Review. Emily leads workshops as an affiliate of the Amherst Writers & Artists Method. More at emilystoddard.com.